A Parent's Guide to Understanding Math Education in Today's Schools

Cathrine Kellison

Catherine Twomey Fosnot

ISBN:1480272396
ISBN-13: **978-1480272392**

DEDICATION

This book and related DVD are dedicated to Cathrine Kellison and her family. After a long and bravely-fought battle with cancer, Cathrine peacefully left this earth before the materials could be published. May these materials remain in her stead as a testament to her passion for learning and her gift as a writer and filmmaker to say just the right thing, in the right way, to the right audience, at the right time.

ACKNOWLEDGMENTS

This material was supported in part by the National Science Foundation under Grant No. 9911841. Any opinions, findings, and conclusions or recommendations expressed in these materials are those of the authors and do not necessarily reflect the views of the National Science Foundation. The authors gratefully acknowledge the support of the National Science Foundation.

Dear Parents and Families....

We are living in a changing world.

The best gift we can give our children is a good education. We may have had a good education ourselves, or we may have wished for a better one. But, no matter what our own past experiences were with schooling, we all agree that education is valuable. We all want our children to get the best education possible to prepare them for their future. But the world is changing. How do we keep up? What do our children need to learn to be successful in years to come? Are the basics the same?

Our busy lives increasingly demand mental math competency – especially the ability to make quick calculations without using paper and pencil or a calculator. We use mental math in every part of our daily lives - shopping for groceries, checking a bill, figuring out the savings on a sweater that's on sale. We use mental math when the numbers are easy enough to do the calculation in our heads –and even when estimating if an answer on the calculator is right.

Calculators are valuable tools. In today's world, having a calculator is really useful, especially when numbers are large and messy (like computing long columns and doing budgets). If we need paper and pencil to do the arithmetic, we might as well reach for the handheld calculator—it's there, too! This fact alone requires schools to place more emphasis on the development of mental math strategies and number relationships.

The most important instructional goal for our children today is to help them learn to think. Research over the last twenty years shows that creative problem solving and deep understandings of the big ideas behind the math procedures are the building blocks that kids need to be successful with algebra later.

Math education is changing!

Schools are now held to high national standards and these are resulting in new standardized state tests. In 2010, the Common Core State Standards initiative published a set of national standards for mathematics instruction. All but 2 states (Virginia and Texas) adopted them and are now developing new assessments aligned with these standards. The new assessments will be given in 2014. If you want to know more about these standards, including what your child is expected to be able to do in each grade, go to http://www.corestandards.org/.

Classrooms today often look different than what we remember. How can we help our children succeed when the goals of instruction seem so different from what we experienced? This is especially true in math. Today the focus is more on conceptual *understanding*. Most of us probably experienced math lessons where teachers focused on *procedures* and we practiced them. We may be able to do arithmetic with pencil and paper quite well, but do we truly understand why the procedures work? Are we competent in estimating, seeing patterns, problem solving, and using mental math strategies to compute?

Math education today...

- **Encourages students** to explore why procedures work and to find various strategies for solving a problem and to examine each strategy for its efficiency.
- **Allows teachers** to work more closely with students, one-on-one and in groups, discussing and questioning and refining their strategies.
- **Supports students** to work collaboratively with one another, in pairs and groups, to look at options, and to exchange ideas and develop ways to communicate and defend their ideas.
- **Supports children to persevere in solving problems** and to appreciate puzzlement and the fun of "cracking" a problem.
- **Makes the mathematical connection** between the classroom ideas and the real world in which children and their teachers and families live and work.
- **Emphasizes clever mental math computation** and focuses to a lesser degree on pencil and paper arithmetic strategies.
- **Encourages children to model problems**, for example with arrays, ratio tables, and number lines.

In classrooms today, children are being challenged to think, to wonder, to explore, to pose and solve problems about their real world, to craft arguments to defend their thinking, and to use mental math strategies. They are being encouraged to be young mathematicians at work!

Traditionally, arithmetic was often taught as if there was "just one way to do it." Teachers would explain the procedure (like adding and carrying over, or long division) and students would practice it, trying to grasp what the teacher was explaining. Learners were rarely allowed to take the numbers apart in their own ways. Yet, problem solving and playing with number relationships are at the *heart* of what mathematicians do.

Doing mathematics can be like solving a mystery. Math is exciting and creative, and it's also very personal. Each mathematician looks at a problem differently. He or she examines a range of strategies for efficiency, elegance, and ability to model and solve the problem – and others like it. They write up their solutions and proofs to convince each other. Even computation is done creatively. Anne Dowker (1992), a researcher at the University of Oxford, examined the computation strategies of 44 professional mathematicians and found that they used the standard strategies we learned and practiced in school only about 4% of the time when they did arithmetic! Mostly they pulled the numbers apart and used creative mental math strategies. They tinkered with the numbers and they found this "tinkering" fun! Rarely did elementary schooling provide us with opportunities like this—to really *do* mathematics. Usually it was about doing the teacher's problem in the teacher's way. And when the teacher's way didn't make sense, math anxiety was the result.

How real is math anxiety?

Have you ever heard someone say, "I hate math?" or "I'm terrible at math?" But no one ever says, "I hate to read. I never could read." In the Unites States, 4 out of every 10 adults deal with "math anxiety" every day (Lester 2005). Why so many?

One reason is our early math experience. Some of us may look back to grade school and say, "The ways I learned math in school work just fine for me." But those old ways of teaching math *didn't* work for most of the population. In fact, when compared to students in other industrial countries, American students score close to the bottom on problem solving tests! This fact alone is evidence for a need for reform in math education.

What is your mental math ability like? Do you only know one way to add, one way to subtract, one way to multiply, and one way to divide? Many people are in the same boat. Mental math strategies and numeracy were seldom emphasized when we went to school.

Learning involves feelings, too. A high correlation exists between attitude and success in mathematics (Cornell 1999). We tend to associate a bad feeling with a failure. When it comes to math, many adults feel frustrated, angry, embarrassed, bored, and helpless. We could pass these feelings along to our kids without even knowing it. Like us, when instruction is not developmentally-appropriate, children can easily feel this failure, too, and can sometimes just give up. Some parents may try to help their child feel better by saying, "I was never very good at math either." But this statement does more harm than good and can have disastrous effects in the long run.

How do children learn?

Children learn best when they build on what they already know. When your child first learned to ride a bike, her learning was progressive: first, training wheels, balance, and confidence; then came a two-wheeler with its challenges. Finally, she had the skill and confidence for a ten-speed. Explanations or modeling how to ride a bike did not help. She had to learn by figuring it out in her own way but with support, and by doing. It was the same when she learned to walk.

Learning math is no different. Working patiently with your child in ways that are right for his development is better than trying to explain <u>your</u> ways of doing it. Invite him to take numbers apart – in ways that make sense to **him**. Encourage him to calculate his way first – before you direct him toward the standard ways that are familiar to <u>you</u>. Constance Kamii and Anne Dominick (1998), two researchers from the University of Alabama, provide evidence that when children are shown standard carrying and regrouping strategies too early, and asked to use them, they give up trying to understand why they work. Worse, they use them in place of other mental math strategies that they do understand and that would even be more efficient. As they try to use strategies they don't understand, they make many place value mistakes. They even sometimes produce answers that couldn't possibly be right, yet they believe they must be right because they produced them with the "correct" procedure.

It is important for children to develop confidence. There is often more than just one strategy for a solution to a problem, and more than one way to compute. When children are given the opportunity to explore different mathematical strategies to find a solution that works, they are learning to attack problems with confidence. They begin to trust themselves; they don't give up. As the problems become more advanced, they are challenged to find a more refined and efficient solution. Marja van den Heuvel-Panhuizen, a researcher from The Netherlands, found that children in traditional classrooms by grade five were already developing a learned helplessness. They tried fewer problems and gave up more easily than children in reform classrooms (van den Heuvel-Panhuizen and Fosnot, 2001).

A whole-child approach encourages thinking - not only in math, but throughout life.

General Tips

Some parents are excited by this new way of learning math, though others feel left out or helpless. As parents, we may speak a different language, or come from another culture. We might be single parents, or work too many hours, or have several children at home. We're under pressure at work, and sometimes we bring the stress home. On top of everything else, how can we help our kids? This booklet is designed to help you.

Parents DO make a difference. Some kids think if they're naturally smart, they've got it made. Yet, if they don't get it in 5-10 minutes, they give up. Kids don't know – yet –- that there are degrees of understanding and a variety of ways to solve a problem and that part of the fun of doing math *is* the puzzlement, the excitement of "cracking" a problem. Learning takes time, and parents need to be there to make sure that kids stick with it. Hard work does pay off, and exhilaration is the result when hard problems are cracked.

Remember your child's first step? You celebrated it, and showed your support. You can do the same with your child's mathematical strategy – even if she chooses a direction that seems inefficient to you, this is **her** way of making sense of the problem. Try to understand her strategy. You might find new strategies for yourself...! And most likely, the more you look at problems with this new way of thinking and learning, the more relaxed—and excited—you will become about mathematics, too!

Stick with it! **Relax and have fun.** Math doesn't have to create anxiety, and it really can be exciting and challenging. Yes, thinking this way is new for many people, and that's why we've created these parent materials. This booklet and the related DVD are designed just for you. The next section is designed to help you understand the types of computation strategies that are being encouraged in schools today. Work to understand the basics, and then have fun with the games, activities, and challenges that follow, which you can all do at home!! **Keep reading!**

Strengthening your own math...

ADDITION: *Start with this easy problem. Don't write it down, and try not to think about its answer in traditional ways.*

The problem? **39 + 17 = ?**

Hmm... 39 and 17 are "messy" numbers. Let's find numbers that are "friendlier" instead.

1. 39 is close to 40, and 17 to 20. Wouldn't 40 or 20 be easier to work with?
2. So let's make 39 into 40.
3. Since we added an extra 1, let's take it from the 17.
4. 40 + 16 is equivalent to 39 + 17, so we could substitute one expression for another.
5. Now, see how easy it is to get the answer? 40 + 16 is much easier to do in your head and you don't need to carry.

It's a smart way of doing arithmetic...using friendly numbers, as children often say! And children find it easier to understand what they're doing when they keep one number whole, like 39, rather than breaking 39 up into 3 tens and 9 ones, starting with the units and carrying. They also don't lose sense of the magnitude of the number and so they know whether or not their answer is reasonable.

- One child might think of 39 + 17 as 40 + 10 + 6.
- Another might see it as 39 + 1 + 6 + 10.
- A third might solve it as 36 + 20.

Another strategy is to split the numbers up and add the tens or hundreds first. It's easier for some kids to split 39 into 30 + 9, and 17 into 10 + 7, and then to think about the problem as:

$$30 + 10 + 9 + 7 = 40 + 16$$

This is easier for children than starting with the ones column because they are the bigger amounts and they don't lose sense of the magnitude of the number. We used to tell children, "always start with the ones!" This 'rule' can puzzle young children. If it makes no sense to them, it may cause them to lose track of the total amount, and can be the beginning of math anxiety. It may also cause them to think math is just a bag of tricks, and that only smart people understand why the tricks work.

Here's another addition problem – what different strategies can <u>*you*</u> *come up with?*
124 + 49 =

Some 2nd graders came up with these strategies:

- "I think of quarters. It's like 125 plus 50. That's 175..., or 7 quarters. And then I take 2 cents away."
- "I did jumps of tens. It's 124, 134, 144, 154, 164, 174, take away one. 173!"
- "120 + 40 is 160. Plus 13 more equals 173."

<u>SUBTRACTION</u>: *Like with the addition problems, try solving this in your head.*

$$32 - 19 = ?$$

Pretend you are 32 years old and your sister is 19. What is the difference in your ages? When you're 33 and she's 20, will the difference in ages still be the same? Exploring a problem this way makes it easier! It's also an algebraic way of thinking: just substitute one expression for another! 32 − 19 is equivalent to 33 − 20. Now you can do it in your head!

- One child might take away 20 from 32 and then add 1 back to get to 13.
- Another child might add onto 19, saying, "One more gets me to 20, and then another 10 gets me to 30, and 2 more gets me to 32. So the answer is 13."

What strategies can you use to solve _this_ subtraction problem?

300 − 193 = ?

Here's how three 2nd graders solved 300 - 193...

- "300 − 193. I added 7 onto 193, then 100 more. So 107 is the answer."
- "I made the problem 307 − 200. I knew that was 107."
- "I took away 200 and got 100, then added 7 back in at the end. So 107 is the answer."

Some useful tools....

THE NUMBER LINE: Many teachers use *an open number line* to represent children's computation strategies. You are probably familiar with a number line as a line with numbers on it. An *open* number line only has the numbers on it that are in the child's strategy. For example, if a child solves 300 − 193 by taking away 200 from 300 and then adding 7 back in, the teacher would draw the following:

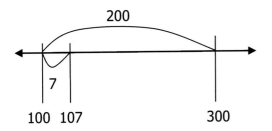

It gives students a visual model and helps kids look at different strategies for solving a problem. Over time the number line becomes a tool to think with. Research shows that the more developed the number line model is for a child, the higher his math achievement (Booth & Siegler, 2006). A number line is an important model to adult mathematicians; it helps them think about number relationships, too!

BLOCKS AND CUBES: Like the number line, children often use blocks, cubes, coins, and other objects to help them visualize and solve problems. At home you can use buttons, bottle caps, and coins. Anything that can be used to model the problem helps!

THE MATH RACK: Researchers now know that babies, as young as we can test them, seem to have an innate ability to see small groups of 1, 2, or 3 objects and know the amounts are different (Dehaene, 1997). It's important to build on what children come to us knowing and that's why it is important to work on making a group of five first. Five can be made by using 3 and 2, or 1 and 4, and the 4 can be seen as 2 and 2, or 3 and 1 more. Building a strong sense (and visual image) of 5 is an important foundation for the later learning of the basic facts. The mathrack was designed to do just that.

It was designed by Adri Treffers, a researcher from The Netherlands. It has two rows with ten beads on each row – five red beads and five white beads. Because it has groups of fives, it helps children use the CHUNKS of five and ten when they are learning the basic facts. For example, they might think of 9 + 4 as 10 + 3 by just sliding over one bead. Or they might think of 7 + 7 as 5 + 2 + 5 + 2. This double can then be learned as 10 + 4, an easier fact for children than 7 + 7, because of place value. You can find more information on the math rack, including where to buy them, at www.mathrack.com. The website also has some free downloadable information on how you can use it with your child.

It's also simple and fun to make together! You can use two shoelaces wrapped around a piece of cardboard. You just need to string 20 beads or cubes, ten in each row. But make sure you use two different colors and you put them in groups of fives! Otherwise children will just count and not make use of the chunks of fives and tens.

All these strategies and learning tools encourage students to develop number sense, to explore number relationships, and to understand what they are doing!

Strengthening your own math some more...

Multiplication and Division

Start with this easy problem. As before don't write it down, and try not to think about its answer in traditional ways.

The problem? 13 x 17 = ?

Hmm... 13 and 17 are "messy" numbers—not so easy to compute in our heads. Let's find some "friendlier" numbers and start with what we know, and to help let's think of a 13 x 17 rectangular array, like a kitchen floor covered with linoleum tiles, or a rectangular patio made of tiles.

- 13 x 17 means 13 groups of 17. So let's do 10 groups of 17 first. Isn't this easier to relate to?
- 10 x 17 is 170. Let's mark these on the array in red.
- Now we only have 3 x 17 left to do.
- This may still be a little hard to do mentally, so let's do 3 x 10. That is easy...30. Let's make these green. So far the total is 200 because 170 plus 30 is 200.
- The part left is 3 x 7. This is 21. Let's make this part blue. All together we have 221 squares, and this is the answer.
- This strategy is called "using partial products." It's an important strategy based on what mathematicians call the distributive property:

$$13 \times 17 = (10 \times 17) + (3 \times 17)$$

You might remember this property from an algebra class. Children who use this strategy are developing a foundation for algebra. Mathematicians represent this symbolically as:

$$a(b + c) = ab + ac$$

Partial Products in a 13 x 17 Array

We don't expect kids to be able to multiply like this in their heads right away. Children usually begin by adding up 17 thirteen times. Precisely because all of this addition is so tedious and time-consuming, when offered the challenge of finding their own shortcuts, children might double 17 to get 34. To solve it they would then do 34 six times and then add a 17. Other children might continue grouping and double the 34 to get 68, then solve the problem by doing 68 three times and adding 17.

It is a great strategy to multiply by the tens first. When children construct this idea you should celebrate with them! They have taken a big step forward. This idea is based on an understanding of the place value in our number system and it is certainly a much faster strategy than adding up all the groups of seventeen one by one!

It's important not to teach the standard procedure too soon. We used to tell children when we were teaching double digit multiplication, "always start with the ones!" This dogma puzzles children. It often makes no sense to them, causes them to lose track of the total amount, and can be the beginning of math anxiety. At first they prefer to do the biggest chunks first and allowing them to do this helps them to understand the pieces that result. You might be thinking, "But my way—the traditional algorithm—is faster." But, it probably only feels faster because you practiced it for so many years, and mental math may be new to you.

Let's explore the traditional algorithm with another array. The first step is 3 x 7. This is 21. You probably learned to write down the 1 and carry the 2 (which is 2 tens). Let's mark this piece in red on an array. The next step is 3 x 1. The 1 is actually 1 ten. So we will color in 3 x 10 with green. The next step is 1 x 7. This 1 is actually 1 ten, so we have 10 x 7. We will color that in blue. The last piece is 1 x 1, but really this is 10 x 10. We will color it yellow. Of course, when we add up all of these pieces we get 221 again. The standard traditional procedure relies on partial products and is based on the distributive property, too. But note that this strategy was actually longer than the first mental math strategy! It has four pieces that need to be added together, with many possible stumbling blocks: it required carrying and remembering what place the digits were in and that some were really tens! All of these stumbling blocks are difficult for young children when they are developing an understanding of multiplication. They often forget the worth of the amounts, and they make carrying and place value mistakes but assume their answer is correct because they think they did the procedure correctly!

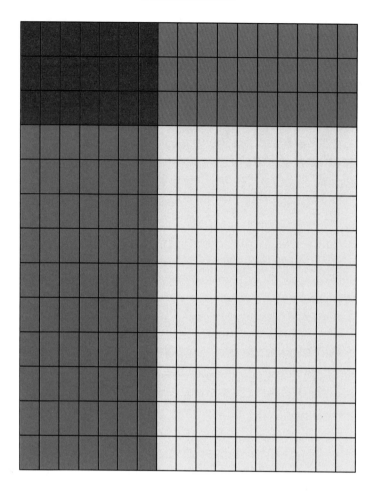

The Standard Algorithm Shown in a 13 x 17 Array

Another mental math strategy that children often use for multiplication is doubling and halving. For example 5 x 16 can be solved by doing 10 x 8. If we double one factor and halve the other, the total amount of tiles in an array is the same. Let's explore this strategy. If we cut the number of columns in half and move them down and then over, we get a 10 by 8 array but the number of tiles has stayed the same!

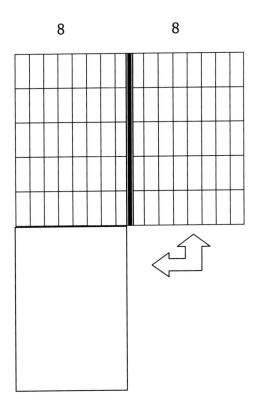

Doubling and Halving

Try taking a quarter of one factor and multiplying the other factor by 4. This produces 20 x 4. The product is still 80, and this computation and the prior one of 10 x 8 were much easier to do mentally than 5 x 16. All we did was group differently:

$$5 \times (4 \times 4) = (5 \times 4) \times 4$$

Mathematicians call this the associative property. When multiplying you can group the factors as you wish without changing the product. Mathematicians write this symbolically as:

$$a \times (b \times c) = (a \times b) \times c$$

Understanding the properties of operations is the foundation for later algebra. There are so many strategies for multiplication! In fact, through the years and across many cultures a wide variety of strategies have been used.

Encourage your child to pull numbers apart in ways that make sense to her and explore a variety of strategies. Representing these on arrays (you can use graph paper) and investigating why they work will develop number sense and help her *really* understand what she is doing.

Let's try some division. How about 300 divided by 12? Pretend you have 300 tiles arranged in 12 rows. How many tiles in each row? Let's draw some easy pieces first in red.

12 x 10 is 120. Let's do that again in blue. Now we are up to 240 tiles. There are 60 more to go, so that must be 5 columns more. We'll color them yellow.

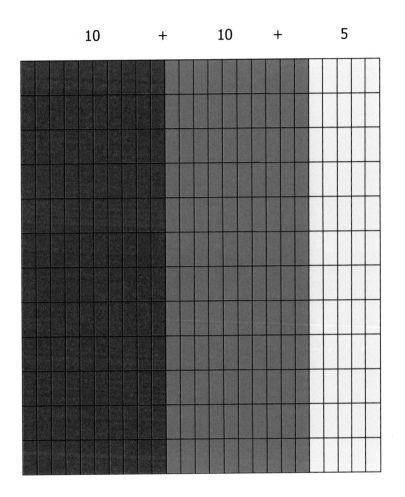

10   +   10   +   5

A 12 x 25 Array Showing 300 Divided by 12

By building rectangular pieces of arrays that are friendly we have solved the problem. There are 25 tiles in each row!

Now let's explore the traditional long division algorithm:

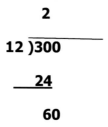

```
           2
        _____
12 )300
        24
        60
```

The first step is 12 goes into 30 twice with 6 remaining. Of course the 30 is really 30 tens. And the 2 is really 2 tens. Did you know that? If not, you can see the problems already of trying to teach children the way you were taught!. So the 24 is really 24 tens, which is 240. Now subtract and we get the sixty. Twelve goes into 60 five times.

```
          25
        _____
12 )300
        24
        60
        60
```

These are the same pieces in the array we did earlier! We did 12 x 20 when we did 12 x 10 twice, and then we added 12 x 5. But wasn't it easier to understand by building up the pieces on the array?

Here is another strategy you might see your child use: If a restaurant bill of $300 had to be shared (paid) by 12 people, wouldn't that be the same as $150 for 6 people, $75 for 3 people, or $100 for 4 people?

$$300/12 = 150/6 = 75/3 = 100/4$$

You probably learned to "reduce" when you learned about fractions. Did you know that this strategy works for division? Division and fractions can both be thought of as a ratio: 3 sub sandwiches shared fairly with 4 people is ¾ of a sub for each person. This is the same ratio as 6 subs for 8 people. Proportional reasoning underlies this strategy. We can scale up or down and still keep the ratio constant. Can you see how all of these mental math strategies not only help children calculate more efficiently, but also are the foundation for higher level math?

Do any of these strategies seem confusing? Stick with it! Thinking this way is new for most of us. That's why we've written this book—to help you understand strategies you may see your child trying to use in order to support and help them.

Try thinking of some clever strategies for the following problems.

228 divided by 12 = ?

22 x 49 = ?

Here's how three 5th graders solved the first problem:

- "12 x 10 is 120. 12 x 5 is half that....so 60. I have 48 more to go. That is 12 x 4 more. So the answer is..........10 + 5 + 4. Nineteen."

- "I made the problem 240 divided by 12. That is 20. That is one group of 12 too many, so the answer is 19."
- "I simplified (reduced) to 114 over 6, and then again to 57 over 3. I could do that one in my head. 19 is the answer."

For the second problem, 22 x 49, they said:

- "I broke the 22 into 20 and 2, and the 49 into 40 and 9. First I did 20 x 40. That is 800. Next I did 20 x 9. That is 180. Then I did 2 x 40....80, and 2 x 9...18. Last I added it all up... 980, plus 20....1000......plus 60....plus 18. So the answer is 1,078."
- "It's close to 22 x 50. That is half of 22 x 100, which is 2200. Half is 1100. Then I have to take 22 away. 1100 − 22 = 1,078."
- "I halved and doubled and used 11 x 98 instead. That is the same as 10 x 98, plus 98. 980 plus 98 is 1,078."

The more you explore the different ways of thinking about problems like this, the more relaxed—and excited—you can be about mathematics. It's happening in classrooms across the country, every day.

More about development and activities you can do at home....

Support your child's development. This is a great time in your child's learning – a time of wonderment and discovery as he learns to compute, measure, and quantify his world. Even at a young age, mathematics plays a huge role in his daily life. His brother has nine books and he's only got eight: it's not fair! Is there enough sugar for the brownies recipe? If there are six brownies and three kids, can they be shared fairly?

No matter how young, your child's thinking is already mathematically complex. Researchers agree that we are born with the ability to see one, two, or three objects at a glance, and to tell which group has more objects in it. Susan Carey, a researcher at NYU, has shown that babies can even do a simple form of addition! In one experiment, babies watched as one toy went into a box. Another was added; and then a third. The researchers then secretly took out one toy, and when the babies only found two in the box, they showed real surprise and puzzlement and they looked for the third!

Although we start off with this early number sense, when we need to think about objects in amounts that are larger than five, we cannot just tell at a glance. This is why civilizations all around the world developed number systems.

A child's ability to count with real meaning develops slowly and progressively. In the beginning, she might copy what she sees or hears around her. So when she counts objects, she might simply be saying the words in singsong and without real meaning. She hasn't yet connected counting with a genuine understanding of number. She might skip over objects, or double count them. She might even count some things over and over! This is natural because young children often do not understand the purpose of counting. Your child may count seven cookies, but when you ask her, "How many cookies do we have here?" she may not yet make the connection that seven is the *amount* of cookies, not the *name* of the cookie she ended on.

Early number sense develops as a child learns about:

- Counting with real understanding, not just as a singsong.
- The purpose of counting. Knowing when he counts, the number he ends on tells him how many, the total amount.
- Starting with a number and counting on, rather than beginning the count from 1 – for example, adding 10 + 3, by adding onto ten, saying 11, 12, 13.
- Comparing some amounts with other amounts, adding amounts together and finding totals or differences.

PARENTS CAN...

Understand that 'math learning' opportunities are all around us in the real world. Look for chances to encourage the fun and the challenges of these math opportunities. There are many ways you can support your child's mathematical development.

EARLY NUMBER SENSE ACTIVITIES

- With your child, take an inventory of things at home and make labels for the amounts. We can count the number of forks, spoons and knives that all of the family members need on the table.
- Do we need the same number of napkins? Why?
- How many shirts do you have? How many jeans or green socks?
- Let's put all the soup cans in one place, beans in another, and dog food in a third place. Then, we'll figure out and label how many cans are in each group. Which group has the most? Least?
- What other objects can we inventory?
- Which family member is the oldest? The youngest? What is the age difference?

Putting objects in groups can be a challenge for kids to understand at first. Can ten (cards) be the same as one (pack of ten cards)? Encourage your child to make counting large amounts easier by making packs of fives and tens.

> **Here's an example.** Say your child has collected 23 baseball cards. Encourage her to put rubber bands around groups of fives or tens, with 3 left over. What does 'left over' really mean? It's a portion of the next full group of five or ten.

An understanding of our number system begins as a child learns about:

- **Putting objects in groups** (of fives, tens, etc.)
- **Skip counting**: 5, 10, 15, 20, or 10, 20, 30, etc.
- **Counting the groups and finding the place value patterns in numbers**. For example, 32 is 3 groups of ten and 2 left over; 132 is 13 groups of ten and 2 left over. [Note: When children are older, they will likely see 132 units represented as 13.2 tens, 1.32 hundreds, or 1,320 tenths].
- **Understanding and making equivalent amounts**. 32 is 3 packs of ten and 2 loose. And, it's equivalent to 2 packs of ten and 12 loose, and 1 pack of ten and 22 loose. Understanding this equivalence is important.
- **Noticing place value patterns** that happen when you add 10 to a number over and over. For example, start with 2 and keep adding 10: It's 2, 12, 22, 32, etc. Or, start with 6: 6, 16, 26, 36, etc. The digit in the unit place always stays the same, and the number of tens increases by one each time you add a ten. This pattern can be very surprising to a young child! You might also explore the pattern that happens when you add 9 to a number over and over.

PARENTS CAN:

Create imaginative ways to find groups and patterns of objects in your child's everyday life.

Have informal conversations about what you've discovered.

More Activities:

- Collect a pile of pocket change, and put the pennies, nickels, dimes and quarters into separate groups. Do any of these groups have enough coins to add up to a dollar? How many coins are left over from a dollar?
- Have your child help you measure ingredients when you're cooking.
- Take kids grocery shopping and compare prices of the same size boxes of cereal, butter or eggs. Compare the prices for buying in bulk versus smaller quantities of food.
- Look for different ways to understand telling time using a traditional non-digital clock. How many minutes, or hours, till we eat, or do homework, or go to bed?
- Using an outdoor thermometer, look at the temperature each day. Is it different in the morning, afternoon and evening? How does it vary by season? Keep a chart.

MULTIPLICATION AND DIVISION ACTIVITIES

Counting groups can be much more difficult than counting objects because the same words have to be used in two ways simultaneously: to count the objects in the group, and to count the groups! This is why the beginning development of multiplication is often very difficult for children. They can't even imagine what 3 x 3 could mean!

Early multiplication and division develop as a child learns about:

- Counting groups with real understanding, not just the objects in them.
- Starting with a number and skip counting on, rather than beginning the count from 1 – for example, to find 4 x 5, saying 5, 10, 15...20.
- Using repeated addition to find the total amount, adding up 4 fives.
- Regrouping the groups, for example turning 4 groups of fives into 2 groups of tens.
- Doubling, knowing that if 2 x 4 equals 8, 4 x 4 is double that amount, so 16.
- Doubling and halving, for example, 3 x 8 = 6 x 4
- Understanding that arrays are made up of rows and columns.
- Using place value, for example using ten times as a partial product.
  12 x 13 = (10 x 13) + (2 x 13)

Eventually children will be able to use the commutative, distributive, and associative properties flexibly and they will look to the numbers first before they decide on a strategy. They will be computing like mathematicians!

PARENTS CAN: Understand that "math learning" opportunities are all around us in the real world. As parents, you can look for great chances to encourage the fun and the challenges, and to support your child's mathematical development. Here are some real-life situations you can use with your child at home for developing early multiplication and division.

Let's take an inventory of things at home again that come in groups and label the amounts.

- **How many cans of soda in 4 six-packs?**
- **How many eggs in 3 dozen?**
- **How many sticks of gum in 8 packs?**
- **How many tiles on the bathroom floor?**
- **What other groups of things can we inventory?**

Look for arrays and figure out how many objects they hold.

- **Chocolate boxes**
- **Egg cartons**

Use graph paper and cut out various rectangular arrays. Measure the dimensions. How many squares in the area? For example, the 3 x 5 array should have 15 squares in it.

DEVELOPING THE BASIC FACTS

What do 'the basic facts' mean in math and are they important to memorize? Basic addition facts are the simple sums, up to 20. Like, 5 + 7; 8 + 9; 7 + 8, etc. They are important in learning math, and getting them automatic is a real necessity for doing mental math. Many parents mistakenly think the basic facts are not a focus in reform classrooms. This could not be farther from the truth.

Teachers in today's classrooms know more about how to teach basic facts than they did years ago, when teachers depended on flashcards, for example. Current research shows that children who struggle to memorize all the facts often don't really understand the relationships between the facts. They think there are hundreds of facts to memorize! In contrast, children who easily learn the facts, understand how they are all related and thus have very few to memorize! So the best way to help children learn the basic facts is to focus on relationships!

Develop the basic facts by starting with doubles and tens. The mathrack can be very useful here because the groups of fives and tens will help.

- **Doubles:** (for example 6 + 6, or 5 + 5, etc.)

- **Facts that make ten:** (for example 3 + 7, 4 + 6, etc.)

Both are important to automatize first. These can then be used to get the answers to all the others more quickly.

- 6 + 7 is a "near double." It equals 6 + 6 + 1.
- 4 + 7 is a "near ten." It can be thought of as 3 + 7 + 1.

  Use the arithmetic rack to explore how facts are related, for example show 5 on the top and 8 on the bottom, and help your child see how 5 + 8 = 10 + 3.

When adding, the numbers can also be turned around. This is an important idea for children to realize, too! Mathematicians call this the commutative property:

- 4 + 8 is equivalent to 8 + 4
- a + b = b + a

PARENTS CAN...

Encourage your child to look for and use relationships between numbers. For the facts that are harder to remember, she can write clues or find other ways to remember. For example, you might encourage her to think about 8 + 7 as 7 + 7 + 1, or if she finds 9 + 6 hard she could think of it as 10 + 5. Work with your child on learning the basic facts like this, and soon they'll come automatically. And, she won't just be memorizing, she'll understand what she is doing— and she'll be developing the foundation for later algebra learning!

Try these math activities with your child.

- **Count out 10 objects like coins or cards,** and then explore the many combinations that total 10. Has she looked for all the possible combinations? Ask her how she can know for sure. Then, do the same with 20 objects.
- **Play games like Double My Number**. For example, pick a number and have him double it. Then pick out another number and double that. Have him give one to you. And so on.
- **Build on the basic facts that she knows**. Help her solve 8 + 7, for example by using 7 + 7. Just add one more! Or use 8 + 8 and take away one!

Developing the Basic Multiplication Facts

Get some graph paper from a local office supply company, such as Staples. Cut out rectangular arrays for each of the facts. You can use these as flashcards, but encourage your child to use relationships and write clues based on relationships on the back of each for the facts that are hard to remember. For example a clue for the 6 x 7 array might be 6 x 6 plus 6, or 3 x 7 twice.

A clue for 4 x 5 might be half of 4 x 10, or 2 x 10.

Start with the squares. Squares are often easier for children to remember first, for example 6 x 6, or 5 x 5, etc. These can then be used to get the answers to many others more quickly. For example, 7 x 8 is equivalent to 7 x 7 plus 7; 8 x 9 is equivalent to 8 x 8 plus 8.

Find the ones that match. When multiplying, the numbers can be turned around—the commutative property. For example, 7 x 8 is equivalent to 8 x 7. You can just turn the array. If you work with your child on learning the basic facts like this, soon all the facts will be automatic. And, he won't just be memorizing, he'll understand what he is doing.

Support the use of doubling, and doubling and halving. For example, 4 x 8 can be figured out by doubling 2 x 8. Similarly, 3 x 8 is equivalent to 6 x 4. With all these relationships in her arsenal, your child will have very few facts to memorize at all! And this understanding of relationships will help your child in algebra later!

Games, Games, and more games....

Kids love games. Board games, card games, and games using dice – these are all fun ways that parents can help children develop mathematical thinking. Board games that use dice and moving pieces, like *Candyland* and *Chutes and Ladders*, are great for kids to develop early number sense, counting strategies, and an understanding of the number line, as the game track is similar to a number line. Card games like *War* or *Go Fish*, and dice games like *Yahtze*, are also helpful.

Here are games from the K-2 classroom that you and your child can play at home...

- Button Track:

Make a track on a piece of strong paper or oak tag. Roll a die, or use a spinner, and place that number of buttons on the track. Take turns and play until the track is filled.

- Tens Concentration:

Take the face cards (jack, queen, etc.) out of a deck of playing cards and put them aside. Lay the rest of the cards face down in rows. Players turn over two cards at a time trying to find combinations that make ten. They take turns, putting all the combinations of ten that they make together. Play continues until as many cards as possible are used. Play cooperatively. For young children who often do not understand the role of luck, cooperative games are better than competitive games with a winner. Add up all the tens when the game ends. This is the score. If it is too hard with the cards turned over, play with the cards facing up. The challenge is to find combinations that make 10, and that should be the focus, not trying to remember where a card was.

- Tens Go Fish:

Take the face cards out of the deck again and then deal the remaining cards out, five cards to each player. The rest of the cards go in a "fish" pile in the center of the table. The object again is to make combinations of ten. For example if you have a four, you need a six. Each player in turn asks one other player of their choosing for the card they need. They have to take a card from the fish pile if the player they ask doesn't have it. Once again, play cooperatively until all cards are used.

- Pick up Tens:

Get together a large pile of dice, roughly 25, or so. Put them in a can. Throw them on a table and make as many tens as you can. For example, 3 + 3 + 4 makes a ten.

- Bag Capture:

On small bags, write the numerals 1-10. Once again, take the face cards out of a deck and put them aside, and play with the others. Each player lays down one card. The card with the greatest amount captures the others and they all go in the bag with that numeral written on it. When all the cards are in the bags, empty the bags one at a time. What is in each? Why does the #1 bag have no cards? Which bag has the most cards? Why?

- Capture Ten:

Get some envelopes and write on them: 10 + 1; 10 + 2; 10 + 3, etc…..up to 10 + 10. Remove the face cards and play with the rest. Players lay down two cards or more until the total is over ten. The total determines which envelope they go in. For example, 9 + 8 goes in the envelope marked, 10 + 7 because 9 + 8 = 10 + 7. You can use the mathrack to model the problem and defend your thinking.

Frequently asked questions.....

Q: *How can I help my kids with math if I can't understand it myself?*

A: You can start by using this book and the related DVD. There are many more materials and articles listed under references in the next section. You can also visit our website: www.newperspectivesonlearning.com. Once there, click on Materials and you will find many more DVDs and books that might be helpful. Your child's teacher is in charge of classroom learning so if your child is struggling, ask the teacher or principal for help. Ask the PTA to sponsor a math night for parents.

Q: *Should I hire a math tutor for my child?*

A: Some parents decide to bring in a tutor if the child's needs can't be met at the school level. But if you do, look for a tutor whose approach to math is similar to what has been described in this booklet. Programs that just teach tricks to get answers, or that focus on memorization or standard pencil/paper algorithms without also developing mental arithmetic strategies, are not helpful.

Q: *Is there a good computer program that could help my child?*
A: Yes. Check out www.dreambox.com. Google it and the site will come up. You can explore it free with your child for a short time to see if she likes it and without any pressure to purchase it. It is aligned with everything described in this booklet and it has won many, many "top tech" awards. It is an "intelligent" adaptive learning environment, meaning that as your child works with it, the program will adapt to her naturally, providing just the right games and activities for her level. There are also free tools on the site that you can use whether you decide to purchase it or not, for example, a digital mathrack.

Q: *My daughter blames her teacher and says she isn't learning anything in class.*

A: First ask yourself: Am I putting pressure on my child to do math problems my way instead of how she's learning in school? This can cause your child confusion because her teacher may be using a curriculum that solves problems in ways that may be different than your ways. Your daughter respects you both, but doesn't know whom to listen to. Explain that her teacher's job is to help kids learn. Each student has a job, called **learning**. Support your child's teacher in front of your child. If you have issues with her teacher, discuss them when your child isn't there.

Q: *Is there research to show that this way of teaching mathematics works?*

A: Yes. In contrast to the way curricula are usually developed, many of the new curricula were developed with extensive research paid for by the National Science Foundation. This booklet and DVD were also developed with funds from the National Science Foundation. About twenty years ago, because of the poor showing of Americans on the international math tests, our government began to fund curriculum projects that would develop a deeper understanding of math concepts and better problem solving abilities. These are the curricula that many schools districts are now adopting. In general, school districts have seen a dramatic rise in test scores once implementation was in place and a few large scale studies have documented this increase. You can contact us at www.newperspectivesonlearning.com if you would like further information on research. We have also provided a list of references in the last section of this book.

Q: *What else can I do, if I still have questions?*

A:

- **If you don't understand how the teacher is working with your child**, ask for an explanation that you <u>can</u> understand. You can ask the principal for a translator if you speak a language different from the teacher.
- **Go to parent-teacher conferences**, or contact the teacher for a separate meeting. How is he doing in class? Does the teacher feel that he needs extra help? What ways can you help the teacher with your child?
- **Accept that your child may be learning differently than you did**. Today's educational reforms are based on decades of extensive studies and research in classrooms around the world.
- **Collaborate with the teacher** in setting up clear guidelines that you can both expect from your child.
- **Stay in contact with the teacher**. Encourage her to send a monthly note and do the same with her. Keep it collaborative and respectful.

- **Avoid personal issues with the teacher**. Offer him your genuine praise when it's deserved. Remember that being a teacher is an important job, and that he has many other students to care for, too.

The times, they are a changing...

This is an age like no other before it. We interact everyday with different technologies, with people from different cultures, and with new ideas. We also juggle family and careers every day. Somehow, we find ways to handle stress, threats to our security, economic disorder, and slashed education budgets.

We work hard – and we count our blessings, knowing that we can be optimistic about our children's future. We want our kids to learn, to grow, and to succeed. We want to pass along our own histories, as well as our ideas and ways of learning, too. But if we help our kids too much, they don't learn on their own. And if we don't support them at all, they may think learning is not important. Finding the right balance is important. The goal of an excellent education gives us the passion to be an independent learner, to make decisions, and to look for solutions to problems. The result is a person who never stops exploring or learning, and who is a life-long learner.

Every day, kids explore new ideas in the classroom. The teachers who guide them in their learning journey are excited, experienced, and currently receiving professional development in the ways of teaching and learning math in today's classrooms described in this booklet. It's important for you to trust your child's teacher and to encourage your child to do the same.

The student learns best when the parents and the teacher work together. This partnership is more difficult if the parent is angry or stressed about the teacher or the curriculum. If you have issues with your child's education, leave your child out of the discussion. It can put her in a very awkward position – she doesn't know whom to listen to because you are each important to her. Students and teachers are each one-third of a Learning Triangle – parents are the final third. **Home is a place where parents can share ideas, imagination, and experiences with their kids. And we can try to understand and mirror what are our kids are learning at school – at home!**

Other Resources

Multi-media materials

There are 18 DVDs with classroom video clips, developed by Maarten Dolk and Catherine Twomey Fosnot that are available through Heinemann Press. These were also developed with funding from the National Science Foundation and are primarily used as inservice materials for teachers but they may also help you understand better how teachers are working with children in reform classrooms. They are each $17 and can be purchased from Heinemann's website: www.heinemann.com.

- Fostering Mathematical Development: The Landscape of Learning, PK-3
- Addition and Subtraction Minilessons, PK-3
- Taking Inventory: The Role of Context in Developing Place Value, K-1
- Working with the Number Line: Mathematical Models, 1-2
- Exploring Ages: The Role of Context in Developing Subtraction, 2-3
- Trades, Jumps and Stops: Early Algebra, 2-3
- Fostering Mathematical Development: The Landscape of Learning, 3-5
- Multiplication Minilessons, 3-5
- Division Minilessons, 3-5
- Working with the Array: Mathematical Models, 3-5
- Turkey Investigations: A Context for Multiplication, 3-5
- Exploring Soda Machines: A Context for Division, 4-5
- Fostering Mathematical Development: The Landscape of Learning, 4-8
- Sharing Submarine Sandwiches: A Context for Fractions, 4-6
- Working with the Ratio Table: Mathematical Models, 5-8
- Exploring Playgrounds: A Context for Multiplication of Fractions, 5-8
- Minilessons for Operations with Fractions, Decimals, and Percents, 5-8
- The California Frog Jumping Contest: Later Algebra, 4-8

Curriculum Materials

There are 24 curriculum units available also from Heinemann. Many schools are currently using these to prepare for and meet the Common Core Standards. Go to www.contextsforlearning.com or to www.newperspectivesonlearning.com and click on materials. The websites are linked. The materials also include 8 illustrated children's books and colorful posters.

Books

Fosnot, C.T. and Dolk, M. (2001). *Young Mathematicians at Work: Constructing Early Number Sense, Addition, and Subtraction.* Portsmouth, NH: Heinemann Press. This is a paperback providing many stories of the math investigations children are doing in schools, their ideas, as well as an overview of mathematical development as it relates to the preschool through grade 3 years.

Fosnot, C.T. and Dolk, M. (2001). *Young Mathematicians at Work: Constructing Multiplication and Division.* Portsmouth, NH: Heinemann Press. This is a paperback providing many stories of the math investigations children are doing in schools, their ideas, as well as an overview of mathematical development as it relates to the grade 3 to 5 years.

Fosnot, C.T. and Dolk, M. (2002). *Young Mathematicians at Work: Constructing Fractions, Decimals, and Percents.* Portsmouth, NH: Heinemann Press. This is a paperback providing many stories of the math investigations children are doing in schools, their ideas, as well as an overview of mathematical development as it relates to the development of fractions in the grade 5 – 8 years.

Fosnot, C.T. and Jacob, B. (2010). *Young Mathematicians at Work: Constructing Algebra.* Portsmouth, NH: Heinemann Press. This is a paperback providing many stories of the math investigations children are doing in schools, their ideas, as well as an overview of mathematical development as it relates to the development of early and later algebra, kindergarten through grade 8.

Kamii, C. (1985). *Young Children Reinvent Arithmetic.* New York: Teacher's College Press. This is a paperback with vivid examples of children's struggles with place value and early number sense, descriptions of their invented strategies, as well as a compilation of helpful games. There are also two sequels to this book, one for grade 2 and one for grade 3.

Schifter, D. and Fosnot, C.T. (1993). *Reconstructing Mathematics Education: Stories of Teachers Meeting the Challenge of Reform.* New York: Teacher's College Press. An older, but helpful, book that describes the changes in math education and the reasons behind them as well as the difficulties teachers face.

Research Articles

Booth, J. and Siegler, R. (2006). Developmental and Individual Differences in Pure Numerical Estimation. In *Developmental Psychology*, Vol. 41, No. 6, 189–201.

Carey, S. (2009). The Origin of Concepts. New York: Oxford University Press.

Cornell, C. (1999). I hate math! I couldn't learn it, and I can't teach it! *Childhood Education* 75 (4).

Dehaene, S. (1997). The Number Sense. New York: Oxford University Press.

Dowker, A. (1992). Computational Estimation Strategies of Professional Mathematicians. *Journal for Research in Mathematics* 23 (1): 45-55.

Kamii, C. and Dominick, A. (1998). The Harmful Effects of Algorithms in Grades 1-4. In *The Teaching and Learning of Algorithms in School Mathematics*, edited by L. Morrow and M. Kenney. Reston, VA. National Council of Teachers of Mathematics.

Lester, W. (2005). Hate Mathematics? You Are Not Alone. Associated Press, August 16, 2005.

The Tri-state study on the effects of the new curricula. Available from the ARC Center, COMAP, Lexington, MA. This is a large scale, three state study on student achievement effects.

van den Heuvel-Panhuizen and Fosnot, C.T. (2001). *Assessment of mathematics education: not only the answers count*. Paper presented at the 25th Conference of the International Group for the Psychology of Mathematics Education. Utrecht, The Netherlands. Published in the Proceedings, Vol. 4., pp. 335-342.

Websites

www.mathematicallysane.org. This website is run by mathematicians and math educators and is the host center for many articles and discussions related to mathematics education.

www.NCTM.org. This website is the home website of the National Council for Teachers of Mathematics.

ABOUT THE AUTHORS

Cathrine Kellison was the president and CEO of Roseville Video. Through Roseville Video, Cathrine created dozens of film pieces including a special on the history of television for the Library of Congress, now on permanent exhibit. Her work has been recognized with top industry awards: Chicago Film Festivals' Gold Hugo award, the Hollywood Radio and Television Society, along with two Monitor awards, a Clio nomination, and an Outstanding Achievement award from Writers Guild of America. For over ten years, she served as an active member of six public education committees in New York City, including the Chancellor's Parent Advisory Committee. She authored two textbooks, and co-authored five others that are used by teachers, counselors, and parents in 14 countries. Cathrine was also an Adjunct professor at NYU's Tisch School of the Arts from 1995 until her death in 2009.

Catherine Twomey Fosnot is the CEO of New Perspectives on Learning, LLC and the Founding Director of Mathematics in the City, a nationally recognized center for professional development at the City College of New York. She has authored and co-authored over 40 books and articles on mathematics education, most recently the *Contexts for Learning Mathematics* series (K-6) and the *Young Mathematicians at Work* series (K-8) with the accompanying professional development materials funded by NSF, published by Heinemann. She also serves as the senior content consultant for the award-winning internet math environment, DreamBox Learning (www.dreambox.com). The American Educational Research Association Special Interest Group on Constructivism has twice awarded her their "significant contribution" award. In 2005, she was the recipient of the Teacher of the Year award from CCNY. She retired from the college in 2010 to devote her time to writing, consulting, and her 4 grandchildren. She resides in New London, CT, where she awakens each day to the sound of the waves and the smell of salt air.

Made in the USA
San Bernardino, CA
11 August 2018